FOUNDATIONS

POEMS

BY

JIMMY RHODES

*"Where were you when I laid the earth's
foundation?
Tell me if you understand.
Who marked off its dimensions?
Surely you know!
Who stretched a measuring line across it?
On what were its footings set,
or who laid its cornerstone -
while the morning stars sang together
and all the angels shouted for joy?"*

Job 38: 4-7

CONTENTS

Facets of Life   PAGE

Foundations	1
Sweet	2
Prayer and Pen	3
Seventy	4
Death	5
Ambition	6-7
Bed of Thorns	8
Kindness	9
A Smoke and ...	10
Author of History	11
Evil Drown	12
The Critic	13
Gas is Gas	14
Work Place	15
Middle Class	15
Angels	16
Life's a Let	17
Late Again	18
My Past	19
Quick One	20
Father Time	20
Fancy Woman	21
Their Choice	22
Commute	23
Submarine	24
2016 Election	25
Sig Rue's Poems	26
Good Ole Gone Days	27
Visitation	28
Lady in Blue	29
Horde	30
Compost	31

CONTENTS (Cont'd)

	PAGE
Song or Sonnet	32
Life x 4	33
Life Cycle	34
Sweet Man	35
Loser	36
Wasted Time	37
Retirement	38
Aging	39
Know-It-All	40
With Your Help	41
The Bar	42
North Shore	43
Trip Out Of Town	44
History	45
Final Fancy	46
Sipping Wine	47
Age	48
Inside Container	49
Facets of Life	50
The Taste	51
"Opened Mouth"	52
Nine Decades Old	53
Christmas Delight	54
Life's Book	55
Pots and Pans	56
Phantom #9	57
Foresight	58
Maladjusted Life	59
State and Metro	60
Null and Void	61
Unity	62
Aging Site	63
My New Steamer	64
Walmart	65
No Illustrations	66

CONTENTS (Cont'd)

PAGE

Sworn as One

Whom and What	67
Memories of Iris	68
Your Calling	69
Done	70
Mothers Do	71
Sworn as One	72
She Loves Me	73
Your Window	74
I Touched	75
How Was It?	76
Pristine	76
Devoid of You	77
Yonder There	78
Another Night	79
I Give	80
Wings of Care	81
Sir Death	82
The Bouquet	83
Forever	84
Remembrance	85
Dad's Sweetness	86
Unbuttoned	87
Each Stanza	88
Teach	89
Old Man	90
The Life of Iris Fancy	91
Endangered	92
Chaste?	93
Eyes	94
Our World	95
A Poet's Wife	96
Technology	97
In Love Again	98

CONTENTS (Cont'd)

PAGE

The Entanglement	99
He Ruminates of Her	100
No Fix	101
By the Lake	102
Afraid	103
Unwritten	104
Cup of You	105
The Wrench	106
Mirror	107
Awakened Poet	108
Alone	109
Touching Her	110

Worldly Wonders

Glorious Tunes	111
God's Word	112
Let's Make a Deal	113
The Weatherman	114
The Lull	115
River	116
Pup	116
Writer's Block #2	117
Your Green Purr	118
Reflections	119
September Winds	120
My Barn	121
Imagination	122
Red Shroud	123
Worldly Wonders	124
White Christmas	125
Past Publications, Excerpts	126

FACETS OF LIFE

FOUNDATIONS

All my life I've held poetry
as an obstacle;
someone else enjoyed to write.

They used poems to
lead you on field trips,
and rhyme to allow you to run.

Now, I often feel traits
of this character;
I experience reading and
writing without thoughts.

I can help a body
up crystal stairs,
or paint an oil
with no touch of brush.

Now, it's a book
with many-a-reasons;
please understand I've gone
all the way.

SWEET

Eyes of a poet like candy
how sweet the lines.
These eyes pardoned as
the hand touches violent times.

Eyes create soft tear drops
pulling volume from a gifted voice.
The magnitude of a mountain vista
stretched with each stroke of choice.

Blooms taste of sugar and sweetness
while sleeping in the nightly air.
Eyelids zipped with the rudeness
of eroticism so moist and clear.

There is filth on every corner as
the gulf blows the cool a-drift.
Eyes of a poet like candy –
sweet.

PRAYER AND PEN

So glossy that lil book
on dusty old desk;
wrapped in such a young freshness;
peacefully sparkling waters rest.

Strong leaves wave
on both sides yonder;
living forever leaving
all dust asunder.

A garden world full
of her blessings;
only one bird
a side dish dressing.

A spring, a rugged wind,
a gypsy of the sky;
all lines designed
to pleasure the eye.

Morn fog thick
as drunken tongue;
gleaming stones the steps
on polished rungs.

Writer wanders, he wanders, the
appearance of demographic lives;
to dust off that cover
and pray one more time.

SEVENTY

I am no longer seen.
In bewilderment,
  at times, it seems.
For many years gone,
  I was viewed and screened.
Eye gazed,
  by watered mouths,
  good enough to eat.
Now, so many
  in this old world,
  choose not to stare
  toward this senior affair.
Am I a different one
  or just
  chronologically impaired?

DEATH

My sadness sponges
the stars from the sky,
the heavenly wait
rolls down my eyes,
with wings set to fly
never leaving the frown,
make the Godly house my dwell
beautiful, entirely and bound.

AMBITION

I have envisioned
my accoutrement of life.

I have guzzled
that cup of ambition.

I have mislaid
necessary hours of sleep.

I have seen
the honey of softened petals.

Oh to hear
the feel of winds thump,
both a blot
and blessing of life.

The waning
of late season to witness
the brown gusts of winds
that bundle
the victims of life.

So admire
that great window of time
that delivers
that cup of ambition.

AMBITION (Cont'd)

Value
that sleepless accoutrement,
that ripening
encounter of spice.

For when
you've lost your ginger,
the spoiled fruit
will leap
from the trees
and mush
at the feet of might.

BED OF THORNS

She gazed through her open window.
Her best friend's car was gone.
The flag was down, on his postal
box, how clever, in deceit, they were found.

A long time since either had tampered,
while under the brand of a ring.
Two wine glasses rest on the veranda;
on a cigarette the red did shine.

Clean sheets held only a suggestive
spot; the room a hint of them.
They whispered, they imagined the
thoughts of car wheels on that gravel road.

It had been several years since
they had discovered the comforts of
sin. But regrets harden quickly like
any bed of thorns.

Through his window they both were inclined.

KINDNESS

The rooster crows with a wicked tongue;
a new creation awakens each early morn.

Take special care the stock of words;
especially that one special bedfellow, I'm told.

Don't ignite each day with trivial matters;
nor speak so early with unkind chatter.

All words each day are linked together;
like close of kin related to each other.

All are entrenched in the first that are expressed;
don't commence your day with a trivial mess.

A SMOKE AND ...

She shifted toward the bar
progressively, allowing little space
in her needy way.

From there, she reached
for a smoke, transforming
from her appeared stupor
to a magical self.

The imploring of her thoughts
were softly received.
Those years,
those many years,
of waiting were over,
accomplishment came upon my dear.

One of acknowledgement
for a unison play,
all good for the other.

Then I lit and took a drag,
blinded by the light.
She moved away
with her satisfied life.

Another she lit.

AUTHOR OF HISTORY

The war machine will not conquer;
  peace is more than a term.

I choose to be the author of history;
  writing nothing of what's wrong.

My pen is the product of peace,
  for those searching the meaning of life.

I'll write only of the good people,
  and delete them when not.

Our forests will cast beauty,
  and storms give off great smiles.

There will only be solutions and reason,
  and only despise those that are not.

We will wander through botanical gardens,
  and never be asked to depart.

So, if your machine still conquers,
  and peace is no longer yours,
my pen is an absolute reminder
  of life, love and the lot.

EVIL DROWN

The event turned him upside down,
no one can escape evil drown.

Not the investor, who's lost all gems!
Not the wife being doubled by him!
Not the innocent touch and the teen surprise!
Not the pastor caught up in his own lusting eyes!

Was he naïve to feel he was forgotten?
Was he just foolish to think evil was not rotten?

Didn't he hear the soldier's with spikes?
Didn't he hear a voice say with all fright?

"I won this day!"

THE CRITIC

I unplugged the mouse, and the mouse I trashed.

I unplugged the keyboard, and the keyboard I trashed.

The computer is made of components, the components can't reboot.

Here is the computer and I in an electronic picture.

When the electronic picture was taken, I unplugged the phone.

GAS IS GAS

My new truck is a wondrous king.
I get confused trying to crank the thing.

As advertised, with all the bells.
Honestly, just an engine and steering would be so swell.

It calls for 93 and never less.
Gas is gas; don't make me guess.

I failed to mention the radio.
This model has a stereo.

I can change a tire, when it goes flat.
Just where is the fancy jack?

I wish I had my old '63,
with an engine, steering, and trusty key.

WORK PLACE

For the gifts, they run many
so different to them:
money, property and others to choose.
In the work place they offer,
self-graciously, one step
ahead in the race . . . .

For me, I invest ink
for the truth in my lines,
the man who has only
questions to comfort his
mind.

MIDDLE CLASS

All are stuck in this rut;
seems a weakened state of mind.

The predecessors of those before
leading the pact to their grave.

Counting, counting their money,
in one hand, stupid as a penny.

ANGELS

I can see these changing days
mostly falling upon the darkest eyes,

of the few remembrances,
rapidly slipping through
as clouds of a turbulent sky.

Away they drift,
not to be captured,
just a few true loves dropped by.

Seems day by day
that dream by dream
fewer prayers are cast.

Are there any angels
actually there?

LIFE'S A LET

No thrill I thought was all mine,
cold filled earth, not spiritual kind.

If I trod over peaceful streets,
evil is pondering and dark shadows seek.

Earth's large let, a guest I am,
to eat, to sleep, to drink with them.

Nothing in me can be surprised.
Her lavish expenses must be declined.

One lives, one lives for world's respect.
Her expenses rendered all past regrets.

One wanders and wanders to past life's nook,
to find the end of a poorly written book.

LATE AGAIN

Their souls have sold out,
that apparition on their faces,
the lights beam and workers
merge their lives undesired.
The train now leaves
that puddle in front,
fast it seems, but not
the stumble of feet a-ground.
A grease stained bag
of breakfast treats explain
the design of JFK's breed.
The Rolex seems fast again.
Could it be or could it be not,
they're tardy again,
life's fast lane starts.

MY PAST

I am accused of writing the past,
as if designed by me.
A work of art, painted
day by day, with my pen.
No
thank you.
I simply slid into
the existing past.
Chronologically, yes,
historically, possibly.
Alone.
No.
When, repented,
I will be moving
along.
Alone.
no.

QUICK ONE

My poems
require a microwave.
They will be warm
and fragrant
when mailed.

FATHER TIME

If only I had known that
he was close, but Father Time
was next to me. I reached to
bolt the door, but hello, he had
reached for me. I remembered
the many times that I was told
to render the doorbell fixed.
He is now in and occupied the
wrinkles of my obesity. If only I
had a New York door, I would
still be young and free. If
only I had known that he
was close.

FANCY WOMAN

Armored in red, her silk fashioned.
The order of corner and bright lights
　wherever she awaits.
Yellow roses align the
　dark trodden boulevards.
She roars and conquered men
　pay their alms.
Naked soldiers she sent to war;
　entire empires have been overthrown.
Armored in silk;
　she fashioned her red hair, again.

THEIR CHOICE

Gray power shines through little shade;
flowers giving off a powdery spray.
Few more leagues to love one seems
entering into the world of dreams.

Long it has been; long ago.
No longer she wonders; just let life go.
Longing to fill their hearts again,
pens and phones track where they've been.

Voices of wonder and notes of steel.
They're on their platform, life's real;
another letter, another voice,
who's in charge and what's the choice?

COMMUTE

In the dumbness of early morning
commute, I whisper an old school tune.

In the grey darkness, my body
finally breeds slight sobering
thoughts of news.

The interstate hovers the
dewy breeze of urban trash.

Dawn flashes through the shapes
of poles and lamps.

Good morning the thunder of the
rooster's call.

SUBMARINE

she was an old tin can,
rather long than wide,
one side rough and one smooth.

half revealed dry,
the other staged wet
when concealed.

simple outside she was,
extra complex within,
could surprise an entire
world.

boom, there she is
   again.

2016 ELECTION

our hearts shattered as souls too rocked
from tube to flask to view and imbibe
news swarms as a moist donkey's eyes melt
taken to non-snobbish offices away
fields and flatlands she travels alone
life ranges larger than mountains to some
policies of reform and internationalism blue
was the election planned what shall they do
deep in our process and in our hearts too
deaths redbud calyx is coming and soon.

SIG RUE'S POEMS

Sig Rue's voice strengthened,
had many lines of life
and light. A mournful pen,
did he display. Through cold
and justice he would persevere.

Now, that voice speaks of a
lighter phrase. The talk of the
day is captured, on page as steel.
He takes three days, if need be;
with pen and paper his delivery.

Bold facts will be his postscript
to see; has only sharpened his love
and dignity. If not free, he will
at least be a mystery.

GOOD OLE GONE DAYS

The days are no longer there; the suburban ones.

The metaphorical end of what was here and gone.

The cell phone connects the dearly loved songs.

The tike's flutter where pink swans spawn.

The dishwasher raps a rhythmic fate.

The sirens sing to keep the innocent aware.

The network brings the software to date.

The blinking clock not keeping the auto there.

The ceiling fan gives the room needed respite.

The dog worries about treat multiple ingredients.

The credit cards help the house celebrate.

The bottled milk containing no milk elements.

The days that are no longer there.

VISITATION

There was a voice in the window
that spoke without face,
just the usual sound of his own,
frightened at first, and then
I remembered the verse.
I had requested His presence with mine.
There was a wonder
of why He was here.
Was it routine
or calendar fly?
Regardless I knew
the image was Thee.
There was a glow
over His head,
blinding the eyes with charm,
no movement, just thine.
His voice sounded bold,
as don't worry, not yet,
this visit is routine.
How are you and why?
I said there were voices,
not of yours, but his.
No one is to trust,
seems our secret to believe
and now I seem all alone.
It was goodbye for now,
don't forget your short dip.
You're in my hands now.
Thanks for your membership.

LADY IN BLUE

The lady was old, I dreamed.
Huge the shaded moon, blue dampened, it was.
As with time passing, it shifts the moon.
The man therein does float.
Tosses about he, as we, helplessly.
The one in blue, the wrapped one, we like to be.
Brown winds depart, rapidly, fading the lady in blue.

HORDE

Anything not being used
is not worthy of attention.

Anything not serving or readily
used is not a high or useful asset.

It is not worthy of recognition,
nor attention, just a leakage
of duty and power.

It is pur-d ol' trash
and an ill-sighted power.

COMPOST

hordes
garbage bags
bags of garbage

masses of waste
gathered experiences
organic matter

breakdown
mother nature
fertile soil

roots of poems
creativity
pen comes to life

SONG OR SONNET

You have good song writers
and great poets too.
The only difference is
the stomp in his foot.
One, two, three, be on your way,
song or sonnet comes to stay.
Both will do what folks must do.
Both will sit here
and drink your juice.
Both will stay and none will go.
Both will sit here
and enjoy the song.
So, I'll just jot my lines
and create the untrue
while my friend stomps
gum from his one shoe.

LIFE X 4

Planes?
　love to fly them.
　show me
　if it flies
I'll fly them.

Loves?
　I've had them
　eyes and legs
　very lil style
I'll love them.

Sorrow?
　let me love again
　let me care again
　to my death
I'll survive.

Failure?
　I'm not ashamed
　I can't define
　not failures
those loves of mine.

LIFE CYCLE

My father passed
   this evening.

Under the bed's edge
    was a chamber's maid
    of last night's relief.
    now a forgotten relic.

With no sermon,
    all that was done
    was vacate the jar
    in the weeds . . .

SWEET MAN

As I travel to the edge of
my line – darker greens -
divided fence – peaceful
man. Well, if a man is strong
and faithful season's in.
Maturation; years on the vine
of easterly sun chasing dawn away.
Oh sweet season, with your
intense flavoring; more sweet
to be, a man strong and faithful,
as the sun draws out the honey dew.

LOSER

What?
You don't have any idea
about the words
I'm putting together?

I only put it down for you
so the title thought through and blue.
Wishy-Washy, I feel
the page not certain
the direction or where to go.

I should struggle on
but only needed to
know the heading, you
say the rest.

I knew you should
pass the test.
For you know it,
all so well!

WASTED TIME

We have lived as we wanted,
wasted shallow dreams,
traveled toward forbidden glimmer,
and failed those that glistened.
Now, we shall lament the grief
that lets to stay,
those hearts that can't be redeemed.
No place to marvel.
No reason to inhabit.
No place to go.
We have lived as we wanted.
The wine glass is still there.

RETIREMENT

How joyful it must have
been for him to surpass
all others: the bombs blasting,
the parade, the event
of desire, and reaching
beyond success.

Others having greater
dreams moving in rather
unified rank, yet so
many lost in the private
room of dread.

Now, as life's done, with
so little time to bask
in humility and gratitude,
while the rear view
reflects the last heat
moving closer to our
equated adventure of death,
with his mind found
in feeble remains.

AGING

That youngish light sets dim
on her bar room face.
Candlelight flows a-glow.
Much there still to offer;
a golden sparkle from her
fingertip.
Her breeze has cooled
from the heated one often
known; a silence fills her
red-stained glass.
She shifts from thinking
about what life could have
spun, to a more tender
moment upon.
That youngish light sets
on her face, her sparkle
flows a-glow.

KNOW-IT-ALL

I know him; a really smart man.
How does this man know so very much?
Is he a know-it-all?

I picture this person learning
so much that he realized
just what he does not know.
This man is humble, in his
quest for learning more.

He is not a know-it-all.
That's the last act
you'll catch him in.
Good for him, salute him,
pray you follow his
earthly means.

He is what he chose to be.
He is not a know-it-all.

WITH YOUR HELP

With both voice and pen,
I am told where we are going:
weather changes, price of melons,
and snacks in the morn.

Daily, thoughts have been rescued,
over and over, these despairing years.
Ideas of whether we shall exist once more?
Am I to be assured of safety from fears?

Stumbling to present an opposing defense,
repeated emotional pain and depression;
opprobrium creeps from untrue friends.
Bless me, my love, with both voice and pen.

THE BAR

Under my brown vase, a bar lies.
The purple wine, the brown vase was
surrounded by.
From drunk, or death, drooped the flowers,
but different was their smell.
Are one the wine and vase?
The lonely flowers done and blown.
Under the brown vase, a bar sits.

NORTH SHORE

I was born on
a dreadful bayou
bank's call,
where blood decants deep
at it's side.

A mecca
to the village beside,
at the bottom
their dreams reside.

Families
they planted fall,
the dredge of the plants
they crawl,
to
the bank's call.

TRIP OUT OF TOWN

We didn't drink or smoke,

but wilder the winds picked
  up our shadows.

Our loneliness gripped
  loose dirt.

Over a long bridge
  we wanted to escape.

Moments froze
  as we sat on the bank.

Our eyes gazed
  at the clear water.

Dark underneath
  we wanted to reach.

We didn't drink or smoke,

All eyes were closed.

HISTORY

Like a nativity scene,
on the courthouse lawn,
under the big oaks,
in Everytown, U.S.A.,
life passes them by.
Are they human?
Did they come to play
dominos or to be
part of tradition?
None ever change. When
they pass, will they
be replaced or will the
majority rule them out,
for the backyard gardens
that grow? They disappear
as all, when history removes
itself. Flat all history
books become.

FINAL FANCY

Slowly to bruit
not commonly known
my thoughts the ebb
tides so alone.

My final fancy
I feel a farcical mind,
so foolish and pointless
not worthy of time.

With no assistance
from power above,
a dredge might render
the sludge of some.

Who would envision
I would famish for,
the lust for hugs
and lips galore?

SIPPING WINE

Did you ever wonder at where are you
or worse, even who,
even worse, there's what to do
right/left where to move?

Was slack to norm
was bound, now free,
now back to form,
was blind to see?

Please accept this tip,
life's better fast to slow,
wine's best if sipped,
so back and forth we go.

AGE

When does the young turn
against the wise, or is
the wisdom not present
but with a feeble disguise?
Are we scorned for life behind,
or just lessened, in statute, while
life passes by? Does the brain
rattle like a diesel machine, or
are the new leaders, of God's will,
rushing a premature despite?

INSIDE CONTAINER

Inside the packaged container
  the Q-tips lined for roll.
In desperation
  a special session.
A quorum of civil servants –
  matching goals and heads.
White here,
  white there . . .
Planning subcommittees
  for manipulations of ears.
A glint
  of what others were about.
Divulgence of all
  so they, in unison,
  grew to resent
  and pardon the other.
Inside the container
  lined for roll.

FACETS OF LIFE

You too my child are a teacher,
one of various and asunder things;
of life and the facets of,
love and the need for.

You too my child are a healer,
one of mental hearted distress.
Your willing rush to mend one's soul,
with spirits so easy to behold.

You too my child are a lover,
one of eyes that pierce the frame.
Lips of satin so moist they animate
to the extent there is no refrain.

THE TASTE

At first taste, I
tasted nothing. Taste
whispered over here.
Taste here was heard.

At first smell, it was
evil. There was malodorous
vapors in the air. Guess I
should have experienced
this sense first.

At first touch, I felt the
warmth of moist tender
skin. The kind I've never
conquered nor been.

"OPENED MOUTH"

The magical tour moves
through alone, or alone
is it crazy or
is an idiot born.
Can it come alive,
burning the deep emotions,
the haze of a dark mood,
responding with bright spite.
Is it home or still alone
with new rules with
unforgotten stories with
no systematic debate of
many created words passing
or tremendous energy wasted?
Does hurt seem to subside,
not true a contradiction of lines
with words untold,
with mouth not closed?
Why do I write?

NINE DECADES OLD

The old man sat in the park
witnessing more than he needed.
A squirrel scampered from the
half-grown maples. He was
reminded of a better time, a more
entergetic one, when the thoughts
were equated. The elder had seen
many creations in his nine decades.
From the car you had to struggle
to the one not.
From that phone with pics,
a computer, and that bright blue pill,
Oh, to the moon or not.
His body kept no secrets, learning more now.
The many fringes of life had
fallen off the maples. Just
a few brown leaves to remember its
beauty. In his sleep he goes, it's
winter just past seventy then.

CHRISTMAS DELIGHT

Cast an eye upon the tree's ornaments,
as their entire bodies turn into
Christmas deluxe.

The drift of a cone
is an olfactory delight;
the fragrance of pine
on huge pillars rise.

Forget the name for
it is without one now;
thank God for the wisdom
of His humble towers.

Cones will soon rattle
and be off on their flight,
to settle and evolve,
your grandchildren's surprise.

LIFE'S BOOK

The book of life, how long did it take?
Was it 1-6 days like another, or 70 years
did it take? Did they take their time,
seeking the shade, or was the earth even
bothered by what was bound? Was it
enough to give a name, or anonymous and
left to question right away? How many quit
before the final page? Were they too close
to resist or too far to oppose? Did they
close their eyes while laying him to rest,
or did they just bow heads as tears rolled
down their chests? The book was written, not
one page to be seen, his life was for
nothing and nothing between. It was for
aught, all goodbyes they say. He was a
good man; tomorrow is another day.

POTS AND PANS

The limb hangs bright,
both red and ripe.
Is it more a choice
or a preference they bring?
I eat them both
to distinguish my thing.
It's neither the taste nor appeal
that takes the uncertainty away.
Get out the pots and roll out the pans,
a blackberry cobbler
is truly all you can stand.

PHANTOM #9

Roaring engines passing by;
sleet and mud covers that #9.
Alms to the men that wear the black.
Another public servant gone.
They ride the big wheels
lost in the night.
Spotted old puppy fixed
at thin sides.
Over the weather
they ride so high
flying signals of rivets
tacked to the sky.
Clouds that once decorated the air
are instant raindrops
from red hoses there.
Down the pole they go,
from their decent meal,
to fight just one more
building that lives with a smile.
Another public servant gone
on Phantom #9.

FORESIGHT

Glancing in my rear view mirror,
suddenly to see my waning life.
Like the brain dividing thoughts
into short and long, only small
things left, as the great have flown.
Will they come before the urn mantles?
Or, am I to settle for this one day?

MALADJUSTED LIFE

Early, to end this sleepless
night, at four. Fan's lamp
back the intermittent fog
of morn. Wife boasting of extended
sobriety with her very well
orchestrated dreams. This insomnia
has sanctioned all pages;
infinite hours, displayed in such
inanimate reams. Coffee, oh coffee,
black tar each fix,
before the western man rides
the moonless sky across such an
unproductive flight.
Adjacently, the wakefulness
offers a sequel to her
impossible dreams; another morning
in a maladjusted
suburban life they breathe.

STATE AND METRO

This is not the page for those that
seek weather, chuckles, or trends.
It's a final glance at a blue haired
woman, a baby boomer and who we'll
never see again. It's almost like online
dating; her picture of 30, not 92.
It's good about telling the final stop,
never missed, only one in town. There
are so many that board that train,
no wonder no space is left.
So, say goodbye to the
blue haired woman; she will be missed
for a few more days.

NULL AND VOID

There is no place I call home.
I don't come to it often;
only three times each day.
Morning to walk no pups,
midday unlimited tofu,
and finally no table for two.
For no installments nor utilities,
it's rather not too pricey
for the three unchosen visits.
Plans are to dwell here
until all assets are null.
There is no place I call home.

UNITY

A vulturous attraction
when she came to me.
A restricted self,
of unusual being.
As my mouth tasted,
the trait of bitter tongue,
in the dark or shine,
with un-winded lungs.
When fate arrives,
but not too soon,
I commence a life
of peculiarity.

AGING SITE

And here's for you another aging site;
wholesome we are, she by my side.

Soft whispers come of worshiped dear;
oh, the brightness of this day.

All those personal parts that fade;
emptiness of a lonesome body swayed.

With arms of oars, I rowed with care;
carefully my hands combed that soft fell hair.

Sharing offerings for stumbling in haste;
to that pond of dowered wares.

And here for you, another aging site.

MY NEW STEAMER

in seconds,
you begin to waltz
with your new
Christmas steamer.
you slide, twist, and bend;
you want to kiss,
a cloud of smoke bliss.
as much a dancer,
as a maid.
from a maid,
to a wife,
and back again.
from kitchen,
to hall,
you go;
like a cloud of smoke.
the new wears off,
back to the mop
again.

WALMART

A post-it, on my truck window,
explaining just how beautiful
I must be to own such a machine.
"I would like to meet the driver
of this ride," it said.
"Please text."
I leapt out, into the lot,
hoping to catch a glimpse,
a glimpse, of the one of good taste.
I couldn't let go; the idea,
stupid situation, but sensual
in its own way.
Somehow the earth was
shining …. spinning.
Where had she gone?
Drifting clouds and landscapes
were different, feeling good
about self.
What a complete day,
but why?
But why
didn't I phone?

NO ILLUSTRATIONS

This book contains many lessons
as such the elephant to fly
and the results of the fatal crash
when not to propel as taught.

This book with its generic cover
for sale on a shelf in an
area cut-rate budget store
no illustrations
too cheap to engage.

This book offers a scent
thousands of varieties
of flowers hidden
tween these shabby covers.

This book is silenced by
honesty and hope, gently, so gently,
my browsing friend,
between the lines the only
pictures given.

SWORN AS ONE

WHOM AND WHAT

The repentance complete with
the burning of the last fires.

The self in life will
no longer perpetually be found.

The love of a single woman will
die and depart this earth endlessly.

The farewell in writing was
forbidden in the presence of
this daily rain, while bowing with
no discovery to whom or what.

MEMORIES OF IRIS

When dark night quickens
  at the edge of town
  and he became aware
  of dampened souls
night ladies sprouting
  resplendently bright
  with each flicker
  of bus stop toll
two aimless smiles
  cover that block
  and vanish around
  the alley site
the star-like spark
  of poise that night
  distributes across
  red roof top lights
he had hoped that
  he would love again
  as he kissed
  her lips away
but the wetness
  was not as wonderful
  as all the memories
  that had come his way.

YOUR CALLING

It's seven o'clock this Saturday.
The rains fall as sheets on their heads.
The heads of the deer in the field,
golden no longer, darkened from the frost.

The house an icy wonderland,
merry with the melody of songs.
It's Christmas in the loving house
so on the fire another log we cast.

It's wondrous that feeling of splendor,
the family unites strong and warm.
Another loss from close-knit members,
Uncle Albert, went this time without alarm
to another place of eternity,
rejoiced by all, Merry Christmas
to those that are called.

DONE

You don't want to hear the echoes,
as well as I not to tell.
Shall we listen to the utters,
as they fall upon our same ole selves?
It's a simple life, with no reason,
weighing fate for life's easy dwell.
My loves to count sparingly,
on one sober trembling hand.
Count, as the past of an eraser,
wash further echoes down the way.
These hinges are frozen;
this page done,
life slowly drifts away.

MOTHERS DO

I was born at 2:00 a.m. that morn.
We were not yet two when
  she started our clock.
She began to take care of me
  the seconds, alive and then
  after the cord herself she cut through.
In seconds, I was on my own.
"That's what mothers do," she said.
She understood that one day I would
  leave her for good.
Flight to the sky
  myself beyond gravity.
Let go.
But I never did.
The cord's still there,
  like the branch of an apple tree.
A mother's work is
  a sight to see.
I became a stem of
  mamma's trunk,
    at 2:00 a.m.
      She said.

SWORN AS ONE

When your interests can't be ignited,
you won't even peer my way.
The propositional persiflage comes slowly,
and physical feet march a different tune.
A lengthy sullen road was traveled:
heavy hearts and cold, cold eyes.
The splendor of the alternate solution;
forgives my rough furrowed face.
I hold one hand in endorsement,
and savor the same old taste.
Your flesh is no longer screaming;
we're held together for what's right.
As sure as the sun that guides us,
God's creatures sworn as one.
Our voices rejoice with pleasure,
arriving at what He has done.

SHE LOVES ME

She came to visit;
  she gave a daisy.
I kissed the flower;
  I placed the flower in my bowl.
My actions a confession,
  my heart her goal.

Was it fair to have guessed it;
  was it safe to suppose?
It was a rhyme in life's lines;
  it was a poem of love.
Every petal was selected;
  every petal spoke.

"She loves me."
  "She loves me not."
    "She loves me."

YOUR WINDOW

My pen strokes white pad,
slowly, all night, nightly,
as a messenger sending sweetness
crosses the newly created route.

No place for the young,
the weak, weaving the wind,
the frail willows weep.

Only the strong,
the seasoned oaks,
tall, with girth,
and age.

My pages are many,
as they mount.
The moon changing
its direction
seeing your window
from mine.

I TOUCHED

She was modeling nothing
but her desire and smile;
a flash of firewood, she glowed.

That scented light exhibited
the finer things of life,
while tongues of warmth
displayed the design.

A recline into the pillow,
the silhouette, I swore
not to touch.

HOW WAS IT?

I had to inquire,
as she turned
to reach for a distant towel?

PRISTINE

How can I, having conducted
self in such villainy,
being in an original
and unspoiled state,
ask for pensive thoughts
of repentance?

DEVOID OF YOU

As I write, I write a poem about her;
even though you'll think it's of you.
Nowhere, in this lyrical effort,
I will you not in this poem to live.

Even though you sit
there with a vision;
you'll vanish before
that primary arrest.

In the splendid method,
I capture her;
will be the ruin
of your blissfulness.

These drafts will
abandon and erase you,
as they are exhaustively
devoid of your kind.

I'll devote other lines
for your beauty;
so batten down those variable feelings,
this poem is always ending
and you'll be forgotten
before you rejoice a rhyme.

YONDER THERE

Her arms as tendrils
securely molding face

Her visual
a-fire kindling soul

Her fragrance as sweet
as pleasant smells

Her height ideally measured
my arms to repeat

Her offal delectable
as a five star affair

Her love leads more distant
than yonder there

ANOTHER NIGHT

So you cry out for the loves
that have lost you. Silence....
with closed ears the world
will receive.

You may tear of sadness,
while red lips soil the rim,
and still drown in the red dye tonight.

Few loves will cross your ford,
through the waters you shed
alone. Be happy for a few more to plunder,
another thought, another body, another night.

You will find this world
a lonesome acrimony, with
many whom have entered the race.
If you must cry out in anger,
expect only one soul to hear your case.

I GIVE

Every day to you
a faint offering I give.

Polished years have passed
with only scruffy leather I give.

My breath I give,
though squeaky dove wings.

Cloudy skies are given
to be worn as royalty.

Blood name if desired,
scattered by other reigns.

The jeweled gallimafries
I choose for your appeal.

Stand with this rusty trophy
and believe it so true.

Every day to you
a life's offering I give.

WINGS OF CARE

I want to live a small life;
open your heart.
I just came from the garden
delivering sweet offerings to you.

Passions of the
sun's golden mouth;
open your heart.
Let's feed the cloud's eyes,
our gift to them.

These garden sweets
I deliver only onto you.
Open up for me:
open your small life,
your wings of care.

SIR DEATH

Several others, because they did not see,
that sworn legal vow, close friend to me.
Yet, then I glare at Sir Death's face
and dream of life's eternal pace.
Or when I grow toxic in this lonesome place,
suddenly, I see your smiling face.

THE BOUQUET

That special morning I pictured
my love grooming
that sweetness of honey.

She climbed
from the footed tub
to reach for the distant towel.

Was she full of morning glory,
sleepy,
or humming a gentle sway?

In her essence
she would fly, bloom to bloom,
questing the nectar of her man.

He was there
in his royal flamboyance;
the perfect beginning
of another day's end.

FOREVER

Those colossal leaves
of the great red maple,
flinging the breeze
across the napkin retreat.

A young couple
plan lives together
beneath those
sculptures of dust.

The provident future they deliberate
of their love being there
long into infinity,
both she and he.

The pair of chosen ones
dust to dust it seems.

REMEMBRANCE

The name of the players are the
first to go, followed orderly by
teams, the score, the regrettable
conclusion; then the entire game
which was never seen, never even
heard.

The fire of a man's lips were
kissed and life watched illuminate
with him. Just like a game, or
was it, when he slowly drifted from
mind's way. And suddenly, the game
was forgotten, even the letters of
his love's name.

Whatever your heart is trying to
encompass are not resting in
fingertips. No doubt that you gaze
out the window and marvel at a
flickering glimpse of his face.

No doubt the game seems to have
drifted from his love poem that
used to be spoken by heart. No wonder
why you misplaced his name;
just let him fade away.

DAD'S SWEETNESS

Today, as we sorted
through the bits and pieces
of our dad's last tools,
there under thirty years
of dust, hid the very last
of his white grape wine.

Perfected it was,
a double take,
ten pounds sugar,
one yeast cake.

Dusted, we found a glorious container
full of his calculated remains,
the recipe of a man's long past,
with sweetness preserved,
wished his last goodbyes
just thirty years ago,
today.

UNBUTTONED

Finally, I came to you,
my dear.
The acts, the many acts
anticipating flesh human,
with you.
Much talk, little preparation
I'm with you.
The smoothness, the acceptance,
of your kind strength.
Eyes closed, silence heard;
I never held you this way.
Unbuttoned we are.

EACH STANZA

In the first stanza
  of each poem,
  the color gray it is,
  in that lonesome home.
The one of dark
  and gutted halls.
I am there alone
  and shouldn't be;
  freedom seen through
  tinted screens.
On a street of stop,
  not go, it seems.
I should venture out
  but afraid, I'd be.
My mask may loosen
  and spring free.
In the second stanza
  of each poem . . . .

TEACH

Seventy years in this man's world.
Many I lived for call me "Teach".
Say yes, oh yes, it was for them.
Laugh and laugh at those tears a-fallin.
A salty tongue, I tasted them all.
I think all my good life did.
If faith extends my sanity for some years,
that word "Teach" will be in more vocabularies.

OLD MAN

Oh lil loved one;
take a look at my life.
Seems he has lost the
vigor to expand his family strife;
the father of time
has taken his direction away.
Older now, than once,
the nights are too long
to dance and progress.
Oh, lil loved one;
that playful young man.
Why did you wait
to deprive me now?

THE LIFE OF IRIS FANCY

At the age of 27,
Iris realized
that she was blind.
Never to see that steeple,
in the courtyard,
nor to wipe
those baby's eyes.

At the age of 27,
she realized
that men resented
her kind.
The desire to be with,
but not bride.

At the age of 27,
she realized
she would never drive
that fancy sports car,
nor have that cottage
in the countryside.
Iris Fancy found herself
on a rooftop,
and could plainly see
that God would never reprieve.
Iris at age 27

ENDANGERED

Surrounding, they could be felt,
yet no form in the distant scene.
Their remembrance replaced fully.
Magnanimous, they had symbolized
an unwillingness, of soul separation,
of yourself, and many other forms of life.
Afraid of them not, as a butte offered,
exclusive protection of this giant.
Acrimonious words, nor other of
earthly manner, could describe
the magnificence of the spotted valley
that stood so quietly, that sight seemed
such a mental effort to touch.
In her stillness, the heart could
focus and hear the deepest wishes
of the heart, as though the brain
and heart were as one.

CHASTE?

Let us go, just us,
  to an evening that spreads
  like spotted pups
  in pursuit of that
  delight.
Let us go through
  the mist of streets,
  staggered shadows,
  sounds of music,
  and wooden dance hall floors.
The toast of wine;
  the fancy pub,
  arm in arm,
  no hands,
  no hands.
Then what
  is the question?
Should we need
  to answer?
Yes,
  the sojourn was made.

EYES

Eyes
with depth of caverns sleep,
dreaming our past away.
Renaissance so pure, waiting for new.
Bring me your eyes.

Then we drift away,
reclining cozily embraced.
Eyes
with depth of caverns sleep.
Bring me your eyes.

OUR WORLD

To live in the world –
in my world,
you must inherit my things:
to love –
love in my heart
and in yours,
against mine,
and with perfect timing,
let go
go to
my world.

Go now –
go into
that chosen heart;
screen not what I have done.
I have made
a sacred place
for you,
you,
the only one.

So go now –
go
into our world,
dream not
that other side.
Go now,
go,
no sin will there be,
go now,
go,
to our world.

A POET'S WIFE

No eyes upon the poet's wife, no
matter how splendid she might
be. Why are poems not written
of thee; such suffering this pen
begins. A set of lovers splaying
along the trail down the tilted
way. They read shared eyes
instead of prose; a story composed
by silver. Light could be poured
into these events; they plan loves'
maturity and a flask of wine.
A loan, just another fable,
the one told themselves. What is
this love and laughter sown in
their hearts? Is it a spiritual
whisper of two souls in love? Why
are poems not written of thee?

TECHNOLOGY

Now I travel from
  place to place,
the dark deprives
  my every move.
With toes and fingers,
  as my G.P.S.,
  a sudden blow
  set my teeth to rest.
We rely on the strangest things
  to find our every way.

IN LOVE AGAIN

I wanted to speak frankly
about love, or will I?
Well, actually the light turns cold
and dark warm.
Do our loves of life imitate
the fragments of pens?
Or art to construct a sky so blue
that only in your chamber
great image of you.
Am I going blind, eyes bursting;
seeing more than is there?
Unshackle the thoughts,
and shod that horse,
the ride commenced to roll.
My views of life, a circular stair;
and in a moment the turn
is there. Again, again love,
in love again.

THE ENTANGLEMENT

Through the darkness, the entanglement,
soul for soul, sent to be.

Lips of gaskets in exploration;
knees sounding a steady tune.

A coat from window's frosty cold,
he wears her perfect fit.

Another night held for ransom,
until death they were meant.

They met on a fling,
just to write through the nights;

a sudden spark and a kindle,
he was there and she kind.

The pen became a symbol
of yet better things beware.

Through the darkness, the web,
two souls attached bare.

HE RUMINATES OF HER

Listen to reason, some set forth.
Reason falls short of green eyes,
moist lips and collectibles.

His love is reckless, unknown;
those who preach say short lived.
He pictures it heaven,
with tongues summer breeze.

Is she there, he ponders,
and he ponders in excess.
Not wise they say; he conjures her space.
Does he only kiss the dark or truly her face?

NO FIX

Nothing but belief for today,
soothing time for the heart inside.

The thunder of a soul to weather,
flocks lost their skies to fly.

One can't count the coldness surrounds,
no soul, no heart, no fix.

BY THE LAKE

Is better to linger here
   by the lake,
right here on rain baked
   beach.

Much quietness as the
   two of we,
in calm and deepest
   word.

Love like strings
   of a banjo,
too many chords
   to count.

AFRAID

The swallows dart our skies,
harmonious our bodies lie, they lie.

While kindling powers our stove,
we touch as eyes close, they close.

Warmth we share mouth to mouth;
directions change north to south.

Covers tumble, chill sneaks;
love encroaches cheek to cheek.

Evening passes, several parades;
morning strangers afraid, afraid.

UNWRITTEN

My hands reach for her body;
touching places I've often desired.

Acts of the minds I want to digest;
closer to divine what wants to be mine.

For weeks thoughts linger;
their demise lives like ours.

Still only remembrance of that
cold unwritten desire.

CUP OF YOU

It was the end of a long dinner;
there was more than just wine to come.
Combining two, as one sparkling soul,
with the glow of a single torch.
A smoke drift cirrus it forms,
drifting across the veranda porch.
Meeting ones heralded fingers ring
still wet from the exotic swim,
the pen, there, in hand I would
light another up, after having
a taste of coffee, and a hot cup of you.

THE WRENCH

Mom was terribly thin by choice.
Like prison bars, her family closed in.
To keep law and order she could be mean.
Her blue-veined hands were soft and clean.
Mom was terribly thin by choice,
held against our face, as we fell ill.
Mom was terribly thin by choice.
Like prison bars, her family closed in.

MIRROR

She stands in front
   of her wishing glass;
oh, the wealth of those
   eyes sparkling.

Now, ain't she sweet
   and honest;
she lets the mirror
   reflect the truth.

So many years
   its job's been done;
from head to toe
   it travels.

Been kissin' back and smiling
   at its feat;
wish I was her
   wishing glass.

Not to pass those
   red kissin' lips;
sitting on the stand
   for me.

AWAKENED POET

The lamp beams on the wall, love.
  The blades thump their reflective frown.
Life displays your waning age, love.
  Darkness bares your feathered hair.
The presents are shadowed by blankets, love,
  with coldness crisp air abounds.

I sing you a lullaby, love.
  Your dreams are sure to come.
This is sure to be Nature's Walk, love,
  the elite is yet to be.
The darkness guides the shepherd, love.
  He sees oer his flock so well.

The whole world in a rejoiceful mode, love,
  the holy night has ceased your reign.
The sunlight will soon be heard, love,
  and on its way be springing.
Your loving poet is still awake, love.
  This one is still around.

ALONE

Never obligated to be shown,
down that dark path sole alone.

Too vain for idle relief,
the marcher surely to encounter grief.

He travels the road unknown,
that parts the trees and nature roams.

A futile attempt to comfort the need,
to have a partner for his self-esteem.

TOUCHING HER

That path of the morning
so moist on human rust.
Sounds only of distant nature
voicing along the guided way.

The sky broad and blue falls
gently over bed's edge.
Glistens of spider webs sparkle
as the engineer floats along.

Guided down that open path,
a muted ventriloquist leads the way.
Darkness, freshness the natural
thrill, to touch her is so serene.

So kingly the feeling,
with the touch of queen's wares.
A glass world to be shaken
until reality opens them again.

WORLDLY WONDERS

GLORIOUS TUNES

A monarch it was
that fluttered noses
of his mom's flourishing poses.
To catch one,
a child's dream,
he chased with no means.

A rush,
toward the back kitchen bound
for a trap container
to be found,
of glass,
that Mason jar,
through open door he ran.
His great tumble
the result of haste, he found.

Blood, the sight,
seemed not to slow,
flowing dearly
down legs below.
The scar,
a peculiar shape,
still crawls across
his human cape.

The story telling a fable
of both joy and pain;
only in a childhood
can we reminisce
such glorious tunes.

GOD'S WORD

And what is it you need
to write my poems?

The imagination of a stalled goat,
feed him knowledge,
hobble to the pad,
whisper in his ear,
hand him my pen,
he will write.

Pray
and he will excel.

LET'S MAKE A DEAL

Another attempt at a lyrical effort
   but where are the words?
My vacant dictionary
   renders emptiness.
Are the words comforting
   the rabbit in my hat?
Spring break in La Florida,
   melanin closing in.

But, oh look,
   a few in the pocket,
   both nouns
   moon and stars.

So, I sit with my folder
   in a rage of pressure.
Just for the heck of it
   or fun
     I dictate pen's behest.
I speak to the hail
   melt like tears of fire.
I speak to my pup
   I love you
   for a lick.
I speak to nature
   on a sandy beach
   roll tide roll
   roll back
   only ripples seen.

I only clench the pen
   so what is to be done?
I pray
   pen in flight
   so . . . .
   let's make a deal.

THE WEATHERMAN

It should be raining outside; it's 8:00 a.m.,
we expected 40% by then.
I don't know about the weatherman.
It should be raining, but not a cloud in our sky.
I love to write about the rain on foliage, so
bright;
maybe by noon we can expect a change.
I don't know about the weatherman;
we expected 40% by now.

THE LULL

A poem starts out as a lone lover,
orienting into darkness of storm,
angling into the rain, shielding face,
from the regrets, of lost loves dragging behind.

The commuter persists in his misery,
wading all night, into the fall;
leaving a uniform track of footprints,
along the bewildered shore.

Writing formed by bare branches,
his retched body a biography.
Every lost love a proper noun,
at dawn's transitional care.

Some poems end without solutions,
but every storm has its temporary claim.

RIVER

Like a river,
my pen has unsure boundaries;
It just runs.

PUP

The voice of my pen,
how it has longed
to speak to my pups.

WRITER'S BLOCK #2

A corn seedling trying to
sprout through the crusty sand
after a pounding rain

struggles with the hard earth
but finds it impossible
to start it's new life.

YOUR GREEN PURR

I wanted to speak
in stanza
of our dream in unison;
those green eyes sparkled
with campfire glow.

Sorry,
I was not the teller
of the story,
but merely a symbol
of the plot.

In the mist
of that darkened eve,
with the crickets adjourned,
the brightness of stars
trembled bye.

I was less surprised
at the symphony
of the dream,
than the bursts
of life expressed
by your green purr.

REFLECTIONS

Ten months passed; season's gone.
  Pains of cold and hot,
  running down the falls.
  no-help, no-help!

Tears failed to cleanse the past.
  Ten months consumed, droughted
  fields lose will to grow.
  no-help, no-help!

Clouds cover all quickly as sin.
  So why the need so deeply
  instilled?
  no-help, no-help!

Time, very little; a bald man,
  slick without withers, running short
  feel of winter's chill.
  no-help, no-help, no-help!

SEPTEMBER WINDS

Scallop
shells down rippled sand coast
endless visual miles
only polluted summer wear

Offshore
tar drenched
sharks lurk
under pay-to-catch a fish
buffet swim

Is anyone to clean these wonders
or just September's natural
winds stroke
100's of years more?

MY BARN

The smell, the aroma,
the gambrel's fabulous scent,

the wet wood, half eaten,
float that horse's teeth,

the manure, a bouquet,
rolled oats, into a ball
of seeds, tender buds,

the hay, that alfalfa,
a leguminous plant,
so green, so rich,

the bale, a flake taken,
gathered dust, from field

the sudden peck that rooster,
another palm full,
and breakfast you'll poach,

the sounds, those wonders,
as vivid as the smell,
to love, that barn,
visit early, heaven's scent.

IMAGINATION

We go much as a dog's day,
climbing mountains of rocks,
sniffing the way of proverbial knocks.

Disagreeable and disgust,
the semantics of smell,
endless the move,
with mangled tail.

How nice to appear,
a reason or rhyme,
a never ending rat race
to another day's decline.

Imagination?

RED SHROUD

The Red Bird dressed
in her finest Red Bird shroud,
hoping to sit
on her Red Bird fence.

It lets there
both morn and eve,
lusting for that special kiss
from a long lost friend.

Oh, that love
that red, red one,
so deep in love
she was.

He never knew the loveliness
of that bird, and adored
the smile of that red,
red one.

WORLDLY WONDERS

Many have lived with lonely.
Many are misunderstood.
Many have bid riddance to beauty.

But oh, my lady,
your comforts are great.
Your hands warm
as your beating heart.

Oh, the tender motions,
of this existing life:
those rushing brooks,
the face of a morning glory
open to get another breath
of life's journey.

How fortunate our
worldly wonders are.

A WHITE CHRISTMAS

her eyes gazed
out

my white window
seal

white snow fell
covering

the white trees
ground

Previous Publications

Prayer and Pen, July 6, 2019
Nature's Walk, November 30, 2019

EXCERPTS

*Wish I was a ladybug,
for in your garden I would be.*

*This love of mine for the beauty in things,
as a child I have fondled and seen.*

*Summer has passed now,
only sober clouds to see.*

*She is a winter's wind,
as frosty as her flight.*

*I wish I knew the chances,
stranger, you and I.*

*Life is not a paragraph,
but for us two an entire meant to be.*

*Someday, in another time, I pray
to focus one eye on her and the
other on a table for two.*

Made in the USA
Coppell, TX
16 July 2022